With love from rkg

Meditations for a Richer Life of Faith

A Touch of His Presence

with Original Photographs by

Charles Stanley

ZONDERVAN™

GRAND RAPIDS, MICHIGAN 49530 USA

We want to hear from you. Please send your comments about this book to us in care of the address below. Thank you.

GRAND RAPIDS, MICHIGAN 49530 USA
WWW.ZONDERVAN.COM

ZONDERVAN™

A Touch of His Presence
Copyright © 2002 by Charles F. Stanley

Requests for information should be addressed to:

Zondervan, *Grand Rapids, Michigan 49530*

Library of Congress Cataloging-in-Publication Data

Stanley, Charles F.
    A touch of his presence : meditations for a richer life of faith, with original photographs / by Charles Stanley.
       p. cm.
    ISBN 0-310-21494-7
    1. Christian life—Meditations. I. Title.
BV4501.3 S735 2002
242—dc21   2002010804
                                              CIP

This edition printed on acid-free paper.

Interior design by Sherri L. Hoffman

Printed in the United States of America

---

02 03 04 05 06 07 08 / ❖ DC/ 10 9 8 7 6 5 4 3 2 1

---·◆·---

*It is with a heart of gratitude that
I dedicate this book to our In Touch direc-
tors in New Zealand, Don and Jennie Hay.
With great encouragement, diligence, and
financial investment, this wonderful couple
has planted and cultivated the seed
of ministry, which is now growing
to cover their beautiful homeland.*

Contents

Photographs

———— ❖ ————

Acknowledgments

I am deeply indebted to Jim Daily, my longtime friend, who assisted in the preparation of *A Touch of His Presence*, as well as the previous seven volumes in this series.

Introduction

The "Presence."

This is the way the Lord referred to himself in a conversation with Moses, the man of God: "My Presence will go with you, and I will give you rest" (Exodus 33:14). For the Hebrews of old, and for the believer today, it is the very presence of God that marks us as his own.

Indwelt now by the Holy Spirit, all of life is lived in what the ancients called "coram deo," before the face of God. We live, eat, work, pray, weep, and rejoice in the presence of our Lord and Savior Jesus Christ.

The presence of God is a

- Loving presence
- Gentle presence
- Holy presence
- Guiding presence
- Renewing presence
- Saving presence
- And more

"Called into ... fellowship" (1 Corinthians 1:9), the believer can enjoy intimate, sweet fellowship with the Savior. He is our "ever-present help" (Psalm 46:1) who encourages, blesses, and sustains us in our journey of faith.

It is my prayer that *A Touch of His Presence* brings you face-to-face with the reality of God's personal love and care for you. I hope these truths of Scripture bring renewed awareness that God is not only for you, but with you.

His presence makes all the difference.

A Touch of
His Presence

Then the man and his wife heard the sound of the LORD God as he was walking in the garden.

GENESIS 3:8

Paradise Lost and Regained

———— ❁ ————

In the beginning, Adam and Eve did live in Paradise. That place of perfection wasn't really about their surroundings, as beautiful and peaceful as they were. It wasn't about their life together, as harmonious as their relationship initially was.

What made the beginning of life on earth so wonderful was the communion Adam and Eve shared with the Creator. They experienced the presence of God in bliss and intimacy. God talked with them and they spoke freely with him. There was no guilt, no shame, no pretense, no violence, no injustice. God reigned and Adam and Eve tended the garden he had created just for them. It was heaven on earth

The imagery of intimacy abounds. Adam and Eve often heard the "sound of the Lord" as he "walked" through their garden spot. I don't know what that sound must have resembled— maybe it was like leaves rustling with a divine breeze—but it was a familiar sound they knew well. A welcomed sound, a blessed presence.

But one day, after devastating disobedience, they "hid from the Lord." Sin had brought death into the world, but it did far worse; it corrupted intimate fellowship with God as he "drove the man out" from the garden (Genesis 3:24).

Communion with the Father was severed. Unbroken fellowship with the Creator was lost. The rest of the Bible and the constant refrain of mankind ever since has been the quest for paradise regained, the restoration of fellowship with the Creator.

Astoundingly, the seeking heart of the Father has made it possible to experience the wonder of divine communion, the delight of God's constant presence. Through Christ, the Redeemer, our sins are forgiven, the Spirit sent, and our relationship with the Creator restored. We can know Christ personally, experientially, and he knows us.

We were made to live in the presence of God. As St. Augustine said, "Our hearts are restless until they find their rest in Thee." The created order must wait until Christ's return to go back to its original, unspoiled splendor, but we can enjoy the fellowship of God's loving presence in the here and now.

Is there a longing in your heart to sense the touch of the Savior? Do you want to live in the light of his presence? God has made it all possible through the mediating work of Christ, who has reconciled us to the Father and repaired the breach between God and man. All of life can now be lived *coram deo*, in the presence of God.

There is no better place.

---◦---

Lord, I do want to know you more intimately and passionately day by day. Thank you that you have pursued me with your love in order that I might enjoy satisfying fellowship with you. Help me keep this as my focus and goal that I might find my greatest satisfaction in knowing you.

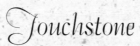

Touchstone

Fellowship with Christ
is paradise regained.

The virgin . . . will call him Immanuel.

ISAIAH 7:14

Immanuel

The prophet Isaiah captured the heart of God's eternal purpose in sending his son to the tiny village of Bethlehem. "Therefore the LORD himself will give you a sign: The virgin will be with child and will give birth to a son, and will call him Immanuel" (Isaiah 7:14).

Seven hundred years later, Joseph, in a deep sleep, heard an angel of the Lord repeat that prophecy as God revealed that Mary, his betrothed wife, was pregnant with none other than God's own son.

At the angel's instruction, Joseph named him Jesus, which in the Greek means "savior."

Jesus, God's son, had come to earth to be "God with us," which is the literal rendering of the original Hebrew word for Immanuel. Jesus had come to earth in a physical body to die in our place for our sins. He had come to show us that he was the only way to the Father.

But he had also come as the One who would be "God with us." Since creation, God had a passionate desire to be with his people. He instructed Moses to build a tabernacle in the wilderness where his holy presence would dwell. Later he commanded Solomon to construct a temple in Jerusalem where again his presence would abide in their midst.

This heart-pounding passion of the Father to be with us—in our midst, in our lives, in our minds, in our hearts, in our emotions—was astonishingly fulfilled in the birth, life, death, and resurrection of Christ. In his son, God was with us as never before—eating, drinking, talking, and sleeping as the Savior who was fully man as well as fully God. He was here in person, God in the flesh.

Today, God is with us in an even more intimate fashion, indwelling each believer with the abiding presence of the Holy Spirit. The Spirit imparts the very life of Christ to our souls, infusing our ordinary lives with the never-ending presence of God.

God, in sending his son and his Spirit, has accomplished the heartbeat of his plan and purpose—to live and dwell with us so that we enjoy fellowship and a relationship with him for all eternity. God wanted to be with us so much that he died for us. And the same is true today: God wants to be with us so he sent the third person of the Trinity.

Incredibly, God wants his presence to be inextricably bound with us for all eternity. John the apostle describes the new heaven and earth in Revelation as a place where "the dwelling of God is with men, and he will live with them. They will be his people, and God himself will be with them and be their God" (Revelation 21:3). Hell, at its worst, is a place where the unbeliever is "shut out from the presence of the Lord and from the majesty of his power" (2 Thessalonians 1:9).

God himself is with you today. He is with you tomorrow. He is with you next year. He is with you when you die. He is with you forever because this is where he longs to be.

What an incredible passion you have, O Lord, to dwell with your people. From the beginning of creation, you planned to make a way through the birth, death, and resurrection of Christ to bring me into everlasting presence. You are my God and I am your child. Thank you for your desire to be with me. I am overwhelmed and thankful.

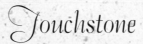

Touchstone

For eternity,
God has planned to dwell
with his people.

When anxiety was great within me, your consolation brought joy to my soul.

PSALM 94:19

Dealing with Worry

───────── ◆ ─────────

Mark Twain, the quintessential American novelist and humorist, said that he had worried about numerous terrible problems in his life, "most of which never happened." His remark may bring a grin to our faces, but beneath the smile is a stark reality. Worry is a debilitating state of mind that if not dealt with can erode our joy, peace, and healthy sense of God's presence.

We worry about our jobs. We worry about our loved ones. We worry about the past. We worry about the future. The perpetual worrier carves emotional channels through which rivers of deeper and stronger fears may eventually travel.

While there are numerous scriptures that speak directly to the problem of worry, I have found the thirty-seventh psalm a particularly targeted strategy to combat the normal anxieties that beset us. "Trust in the LORD and do good; dwell in the land and enjoy safe pasture" (v. 3).

Worry is essentially an assault on the character of God, since underlying most of our concerns is the notion that somehow God will not come through for us. When we confront worry with affirmations of God's goodness, mercy, and faithfulness, we can disarm the explosive nature of worry. When we deliberately choose to trust God to take care of the circumstances that generate our anxiety and simply concentrate on taking care of the business the Lord sets before us each day, we can experience newfound contentment and stability.

"Delight yourself in the LORD and he will give you the desires of your heart" (v. 4). It is virtually impossible to enjoy the pleasure of God's presence and worry at the same time. Our anxieties compel us to focus on what is wrong rather than what is right. When we learn to take delight in the Lord, to focus our attention on him through worship and prayer, we can reverse the effects of worry. The person who delights in the Lord places Christ at the center of his thoughts and actions and looks to the Lord to meet his deepest needs and desires. Delighting in the Lord is a steady gaze of the heart to the wonders of God's person.

"Be still before the LORD and wait patiently for him" (v. 7). Worry creates ripples of fear and uncertainty, keeping us agitated and uneasy. We must quiet our souls, sitting before the Lord for a time of listening to what God says. We must deliberately turn aside from the inner noise and din of anxiety and wait for his input and guidance. God has a way. God has a plan. God has a purpose. He will execute that for the person who waits quietly on him to accomplish it. Don't allow worry to force your hand into some rash act; wait on God's timing.

"Do not fret—it leads only to evil" (v. 8). The Lord commands us to stop worrying because he knows it ultimately leads to evil. We don't have to understand all the implications of worry; we just need to obey God and do our best to cease and desist. "Okay, God, you have told me not to worry. You know I have a strong inclination to do so, but I choose to obey you. Give me the grace and truth to turn it away from my mind and place my confidence in you." This is the kind of commitment that the Lord is looking for, and once you make it—and keep making it—worry will diminish and faith will rise and triumph. Joy will be rediscovered and the pleasure of God will be yours to once again enjoy.

I come to you today, Lord, and place my worries in your capable hands. Deep down I know that you will come through for me, and I do not want to doubt your faithfulness. Put my focus on you instead of my problems and change my worries into affirmations of your greatness and goodness.

Touchstone

God will always come

through for you.

I am in the midst of lions.

PSALM 57:4

Loving Your Enemies

If you live long enough, you are bound to make a few enemies. Somewhere along the journey, you will encounter
someone that seems bent on making your life miserable. It could
be a member of your own family with whom you seem to be at
constant odds. It could be a person at work whose job description surely seems to annoy, irritate, and frustrate you.

In my fifty years of pastoring, I have dealt with a number of
individuals who opposed me at almost every turn. Learning how
to deal with these situations has probably been one of the most
challenging—and rewarding—exercises of my life.

For too many years, I suffered from all the churning emotions that accompanied this kind of personal discord. Anger. Bit-
terness. Disillusionment. I can remember being so absorbed in
the friction between myself and others that my relationship with
the Father suffered greatly. When I would sit down to pray, my
mind seemed to be constantly fixed on skirmishes.

Then I came across a small quote from Alan Redpath, the
former pastor of Moody Bible Church, that revolutionized my
attitude. The Scottish-born minister said, "If you begin with
God, your enemies grow small. If you begin with the enemy, you
may never reach God. If you begin with Him, the problems
begin to dwindle; if you begin with the problems, you never get
through to God. "

What a bolt of truth from God that was! I was incessantly
thinking about the persons who had wronged me, who had
acted unjustly and unfairly, that I had no room for the love of
God in my heart, mind, or will. I was a prisoner of my own

small-minded and unwise perspective. Redpath's words broke through to my soul.

Beginning with God meant that I had to rely on his ability to deal wisely and justly with my adversaries. It meant that I could filter all my negative emotions and ill feelings through his all-powerful Word. It meant that I was not a victim of someone else's power plays or deception, but that my reputation, success, and security rested firmly in the hands of a Sovereign God.

Starting with God also meant that I could pray for that person and really mean it, because if God loved him, then I could too. I can't say that my feelings changed much in every circumstance. In fact, they often didn't. But gradually, I was able to truly affirm the absolute power of the risen Christ to sustain and guide me through these rough encounters.

The Lord is bigger than our enemies. He can use these tumultuous occasions to deepen our faith as we see him at work. Begin with God by worshiping him as the all-sufficient Savior who is working everything together for good. Begin by coming to him in earnest prayer and thanking him that he will use this difficult relationship to draw you deeper into his presence.

Oh, Lord, you know how my mind has been consumed and my spirit heated over this rivalry. It's all I think about. Lord, let me start now by worshiping you and putting you in your proper place in my heart. You are so amazing, so awesome, and I will not let this disunity destroy my intimacy with you. Help me to see you, not my enemy, at work in my life so I may cling to you always.

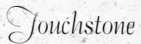 Touchstone

The bigger your God is,
the smaller your problem.

Not having a righteousness of my own.

PHILIPPIANS 3:9

The Righteous Way

———— ❋ ————

Of all the people that Jesus encountered, his harshest words were reserved for the very class of people that seemed the most religious—the Pharisees. Teachers and guardians of the Jewish faith, their legalistic approach had turned God's establishment of a covenant relationship with him into a twisted maze of impersonal rituals.

In a word, the Pharisees were self-righteous and we make a serious mistake if we think we are not susceptible to the same danger today. A self-righteous Christian will rarely experience the wonder of God's loving presence, though he may think otherwise. Thankfully, there are warning signs that can help us detect any traces of self-righteousness before it ensnares us.

Self-righteous Christians usually think they are better than others. Whether in a large church or a small group, there is the sense that somehow God has gifted them with more spiritual gifts, more discernment, and more spiritual maturity than their brothers and sisters in Christ. There is an air of superiority that is easy for others to spot, but extremely difficult for the self-righteous people to detect themselves. The Pharisee who invited Jesus to dinner one evening saw a woman with a questionable lifestyle pour out her tears and expensive perfume on Christ's feet. He could only coldly respond that "she is a sinner" (Luke 7:39).

Self-righteous people are critical and judgmental. Whatever degree of success a person may enjoy, self-righteous individuals are quick to point out the flaws. The Pharisees saw the miracles of Christ, but could only focus on what they perceived as problems. They heard the remarkable teaching and parables of the

Messiah, but they sought to poke legalistic holes in his message. They were experts at calling attention to the speck in their brother's eye. A consistent spirit of criticism about others is only a cheap disguise for a self-righteous attitude.

Self-righteous people look slavishly to their own personal performance, thinking their behavior somehow earns brownie points with God. At the core of all self-righteousness is the belief that we can please God through our continued self-effort. We forget that it was God's performance on the cross that made us—and keeps us—pleasing to him.

Jesus strikes at the core of this thinking. There is no condemnation for us in Christ (Romans 8:1) and therefore absolutely no condemnation for others. God is the judge, not us, for only Christ is worthy to discern. Our only claim to righteousness is what we receive from Christ at salvation, a righteousness not of our doing. It is God himself who makes us righteous, not our feeble attempts.

Ask the Holy Spirit to search you and point out any areas in your life where self-righteous behavior may have encroached. Turn humbly to the loving embrace of a forgiving Father and thank him for the righteousness that he gives freely through faith in Christ. Come back to the place of childlike dependence on the free, rich grace of God.

———— • ————

Jesus, I can never come to a place in my walk with you where my efforts are the basis for my relationship with you. Both my salvation and my sanctification are your gifts to me. Keep me from any haughtiness of spirit that I may humbly follow you and resist any temptation to exalt myself. I only want to honor you.

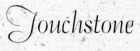

Touchstone

God made you righteous
and keeps you righteous.

But as for me, it is good to be near God.

Drawing Near

———— ❊ ————

he late A. W. Tozer remarked that Christians are too often caught in the "coils of a spurious logic that says if we have found [Christ], we need seek him no more." Having been brought near to personal fellowship with the Lord, the believer has the privilege and responsibility to continue to draw near to him.

We draw near to Christ through a humble spirit. "This is the one I esteem: he who is humble and contrite in spirit, and trembles at my word" (Isaiah 66:2). A humble spirit, an attitude that has a right view of both God's and man's abilities, is an essential ingredient to cultivate a rich sense of God's abiding presence. James wrote that God resists the proud, but extends grace to the humble in spirit (James 4:6). The blessings of God's nearness flourish from a humble heart before him. Genuine meekness is a true recognition of God's sovereign power over people and circumstances. Our heart looks to the Lord to reward our efforts, for what others ignore, God sees and honors. When people are unjust toward us, Christ himself guards our reputation and takes up our cause.

We draw near to God as we cultivate a life of integrity. "The LORD is near to all who call on him, to all who call on him in truth" (Psalm 145:18). Honesty is a straight road to the heart of God. When we continue in known sin patterns and refuse to acknowledge their corrosive influence, we will have a difficult time basking in the nearness of God. In most instances, repentance is the antidote, turning away from sin and toward God. Sin may not be conquered instantly, but we set the course for intimacy when we mean business with God through confession and repentance. James wrote, "Come near to God and he will come near to you. Wash your hands, you sinners, and purify you hearts, you double-minded" (James 4:8).

We draw near to God when we claim our new position in Christ. Too often, guilt over our sins or past erects a barricade between our emotions and the Lord. We shrink from God's presence because we are ashamed of or disappointed about our behavior. We fail to develop any true sense of intimacy. The cross of Christ dealt with our guilt and shame once for all, placing our sins and guilt on Christ himself. Now, as children of God, "there is now no condemnation for those who are in Christ" (Romans 8:1). God is for us, not against us. The Holy Spirit convicts us of specific sin, not to condemn, but to bring our sin to the light of God's cleansing love and forgiveness. We can draw near to God's great throne of grace because we can now find the mercy and grace to help us in our time of need (Hebrews 4:16).

The Christian life is a constant drawing near of our souls to the heart of God. We draw near when we encounter God in his living, active Word. We draw near when we encounter God in systematic, persistent prayer. We draw near when we serve others in Christ's name. God has drawn near to us through Christ's redeeming sacrifice that we might daily draw near to him. There is no greater privilege.

———— • ————

Help me, Lord, to continually draw near to you morning by morning as I gaze upon your wonders and your unfailing love to me. I delight in your nearness and treasure the intimacy of your fellowship. Let me continue to seek you, never becoming complacent or smug in my knowledge of you.

Touchstone

We can draw near to God
because he has drawn
near to us in Christ.

A friend loves at all times.

PROVERBS 17:17

Encountering God Through Friends

---

*J*ackie Robinson was the first player to break the race barrier with the Brooklyn Dodgers in 1947. After the talented third baseman made an error that cost the Dodgers the game, fans along the third baseline began booing Robinson. In that tense moment, infielder Pee Wee Reese, born and reared in the South, came up to him and put his arm around him. The boos stopped and Robinson later referred to that moment as the turning point in his professional career.

Friends are an instrumental part of experiencing God's caring touch. A friend who calls on a lonely night, who brings a meal when we are sick, who prays with us when we are discouraged, is indispensable to God's encouragement. There are times when we simply must go to the Lord for our refreshment, but there are also many times when we need a smile or word from a friend.

David knew the value of a friend. Constantly on the run from King Saul, driven to the wilderness, David found the comfort and strength he needed in Jonathan, his beloved friend. "And Saul's son Jonathan went to David at Horesh and helped him find strength in God" (1 Samuel 23:16).

Jonathan left the comfort of his royal residence and traveled to David's wilderness camp. A genuine friend doesn't mind being inconvenienced. In fact, it is a prerequisite for true friendship. A friend is sensitive to the needs of another and makes the effort to break out of his comfort zone and enter the pain of another.

If we are always preoccupied with our own needs, we will seldom find the rich rewards that friendship brings.

An authentic Christian friend shares encouragement that is "in God." Granted, just the presence of another is often all we need at times and the Lord knows that, but it is also imperative that we base our friendships in the context of Christ's body of believers. David was glad to see Jonathan, but he was also happy to hear Jonathan's reminder of God's favor and blessings. A word from a friend that directs our hearts to God's heart is one of the most powerful demonstrations of God's provision and care.

Moses teamed up with Aaron and Joshua. Elijah and Elisha formed a dynamic duo. Daniel had good friends to hang with him. Jesus sent the disciples out in pairs. Paul traveled with Barnabas and Silas. Throughout Scripture, the principle of accountability and companionship is portrayed as God's unique design for experiencing his presence.

If you need a friend, try something different and think of someone you can help in a tangible way. The very act of helping someone else sows the seed for a future friendship to bloom. Look for a small group study in your church or in a home where you can develop relationships that God can bless. We don't need many friends, just a faithful few.

———— ◆ ————

Jesus, I thank you that you are my friend as well as my Lord and Savior. You understand perfectly our human and emotional needs and place special people in our lives at opportune times to communicate your love. Lead me to those individuals with whom I can fellowship and enjoy the blessings of our presence where two or more are gathered.

Touchstone

Friendship is cultivated
through selfless acts
of kindness.

Search me, O God, and know my heart.

PSALM 139:23

Honest to God

Many of the epistles in the New Testament were written to encourage new believers and instruct them in their faith. But often embedded in many of the letters were rather stiff warnings about problems that had crept into the church. The Galatians needed to continue their walk in the Spirit and not revert back to the law. The Corinthians were dealing with key moral issues. The Thessalonians had some in their midst who were confused about Christ's return and others who were troublesome busybodies.

These issues needed to be confronted if they were to be resolved, which is a vital principle for all who want to make progress in their relationship with Christ. We can deal effectively and victoriously with our problems, but we must first bring them before the Lord, not suppress them.

God encourages us to be honest with him. All spiritual authenticity begins and continues with a transparent admission of our struggles. David prayed, "When I kept silent, my bones wasted away . . . my strength was sapped. . . . Then I acknowledged my sin to you and did not cover up my iniquity" (Psalm 32:3–5). The longer David suppressed his sin, the more his heart ached. Only when he brought his sin to the light of God's forgiving presence did he sense God's comforting presence. Are you looking for comfort? Do you want the joy of forgiveness? Then come to the Lord in true confession, not to be condemned but to be liberated from the weight of our guilt. Why are we afraid to speak candidly and openly with our omniscient Father who knows us perfectly and yet still loves us for eternity?

Sin is not the only context in which God desires our truthfulness. He wants us to be honest with him in our feelings, our emotions, our ambitions, our failures. We all harbor secret fears and longings that we think we can't discuss with God. That's nonsense. Check out the psalms where the writers released their frustrations and disappointments. They wondered where God was in their adversity. They felt abandoned. They questioned his justice. God wasn't threatened by their acknowledgment. He knew, and still knows, that until we surface our complaints and feelings, we will not develop a completely trusting relationship with him.

Allow the Holy Spirit to put his finger on areas of your life where you haven't been completely honest with God. Trust the Lord to give you his grace and wisdom to meet you at your point of need. The solution may not come quickly, but once you begin a heartfelt conversation with God, you are already far down the road to recovery and wholeness.

———— • ————

Father, I admit there are concerns in my heart that I have not expressed to you. For some reason I am afraid to share my true feelings with you. Help me to bring my deep needs before you so I can experience the truth that really does set me free. I know it won't be easy, but I also know your healing waits in the wings.

Touchstone

Honesty isn't the best
policy with God;
it's the only policy.

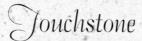

Grace and peace be yours in abundance.

1 PETER 1:2

Into Canaan

———— ◉ ————

*A*t a pivotal moment in the history of Israel, the Lord anointed Joshua to finally lead the people into Canaan. Millions of Hebrews followed Moses' designated successor into the Promised Land and fought the battles necessary to possess the rich hills and valleys of Canaan.

The conquest gained by Joshua is a foreshadowing of the believer's possession of a life of victory. It is the Old Testament preview of the New Testament way of life promised to all who follow Christ. The wilderness, replete with frustration and defeat, is not meant to be the dwelling place for the Christian, though we often find ourselves wandering in its confusion.

The way into Canaan, the Old Testament presage of the abundant life, begins with a perspective of God's might. Of the twelve spies who went into Canaan, only two, Joshua and Caleb, returned with a confident game plan. The ten fearful ones only saw the giants who inhabited the land. Joshua and Caleb saw God. Seeing and believing in the sufficiency and power of God is the first step to an abundant life.

The journey of celebrating God's presence in all of life continues as we recognize him at work in every facet of life. The Lord told Joshua, "As I was with Moses, so I will be with you; I will never leave you nor forsake you" (Joshua 1:5). Perched beside the flooded Jordan river, Joshua needed the assurance that God would be with him in his trek into Canaan. He got it and we have it as well. In fact, Matthew records Jesus' last words on earth as, "And surely I am with you always, to the very end of the age" (Matthew 28:20). The Lord is with us wherever we go, even if we make a wrong turn at times. The abundant life is the very life of Christ at work in us.

Meditating on God's sure and certain promises focuses us on God's continuing presence. God encouraged Joshua to meditate on the Scripture day and night and thus ensure his success (Joshua 1:8). Meditation is a slow and deliberate pondering of selected Scriptures. When we dwell on specific verses that pertain to our needs and challenges, we absorb the truth that sets us free. Setting the truth before us dispels the fears, deception, and unbelief that thwart our enjoyment of the life God promises to his children.

God's victorious presence is experienced as we allow him to fight our battles, as he did for Joshua. Jericho fell, not because of Joshua's strategy, but because of God's power. God himself is willing to fight our battles. We can stand and see God's mighty hand at work as we humble ourselves before him, admit our weaknesses, and ask the Lord to act on our behalf. We handle our responsibilities, but entrust the outcome solely to God's wisdom. We want his results, his way. We refuse to force the issues, but rather confidently wait on God to act, trusting him to change people or circumstances. There is nothing too difficult for him, and when the battle is the Lord's, we can be confident in a godly solution.

God really does want us to experience his fullness. This is one reason why he came to earth (John 10:10). Like Joshua, we can possess its reality by a life of expectant faith, solid assurance of the Lord's presence, disciplined meditation on the Word of God, and confidence in God's ability to bring victory into our midst.

———— ⬦ ————

I realize the abundant life is what you came to give me, Jesus. Neither you nor I are happy with a lukewarm, lethargic spirituality. Help me to experience your life, peace, and joy each day as I learn to possess what you have provided through your grace and goodness. May that life overflow to those around me that all may know the source is you.

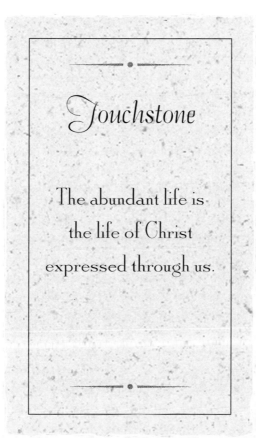

Touchstone

The abundant life is
the life of Christ
expressed through us.

Choose for yourselves this day whom you will serve.

JOSHUA 24:15

It's a Choice

---◦---

hink back for a moment to a high school science or biology class. Can you recall learning about the differences between voluntary and involuntary muscles? A voluntary muscle is one you choose to exercise, like an arm or a leg; an involuntary muscle is one that moves without your consent, like an eyelid or a heart.

As you grow in Christ, you have probably discovered some behavioral tendencies that seem to flare up repeatedly. You always respond angrily to certain events. You talk harshly about certain people. Like the apostle Paul, you want to do the right thing, but you seem to invariably do the wrong thing (Romans 8:14–24). What should be voluntary, controlled responses turn into involuntary, unmanageable reactions.

No matter how hard you try, the problem remains. There is a growing distance between you and the Father. You wonder if he hasn't grown weary of your all-too-frequent failure. You have almost abandoned the prospect of godly change.

There is hope. Intimacy with the Savior can be restored. Spiritual progress can be made. Stubborn behavioral habits can be overcome. But here's the key—you have a choice. The choice isn't to try harder. The choice isn't to rededicate your life to Christ, again. The choice is this: Yield to the ministry of the Holy Spirit. That's it! The solution is voluntary surrender to the enabling presence of the Spirit of God.

Listen to Paul's exhortation to the Galatians who themselves were in grave danger of lapsing back into a legalistic lifestyle that offered no victory over the real power of sin. "So I say, live by the Spirit, and you will not gratify the desires of the sinful nature" (Galatians 5:16). In other words, the only real way to defeat the constant downward drag of our bent toward sin is to yield to the Holy Spirit.

We can't change certain things. We can't rescue ourselves from sinful nature. This is the job description of the Spirit, who alone can liberate us. An enormously high rate of failure is almost guaranteed when we seek to change ourselves through grit and resolve. A supernatural shift can, and often does, occur when we choose to submit to the awesome, ever-present ministry of the Holy Spirit.

"Since we live by the Spirit," Paul writes, "let us keep in step with the Spirit" (Galatians 5:25). Voluntary, daily submission to the Holy Spirit allows him to overthrow the tyranny of sin. That choice allows the Spirit to intervene and interdict entrenched, destructive behavior.

Make the choice today to defeat the power of sin through the power of the Spirit. Ask him to govern your words, thoughts, and deeds. In time, you will notice that the Holy Spirit will supplant your established negative habits of the flesh with fresh, triumphant habits of the Spirit. It's your choice, and his pleasure.

—— • ——

For so long, Lord, I have prayed about this particular habit. It has only worsened, and I almost despair of any victory. I yield myself today to the power of the Holy Spirit who alone can overcome the power of sin. I ask for your help to make this choice to yield to the Spirit each day and anticipate the wonderful day when I know the victory is won. Thank you.

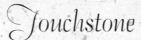

Touchstone

The Holy Spirit can bring
about a supernatural
shift in your life.

Hear my cry, O God; listen to my prayer.

PSALM 61:1

Just Cry Out

---·◉·---

$\mathcal{S}$everal years ago I met with a spiritually wise friend, and he shared with me that when he came to an impasse, he simply cried out to God. I began to study the instances in Scripture when people came to the Lord with desperate pleas. As I faced several adversities in the following months, I did exactly what they did—I cried out God and he answered my intense pleas with his saving help.

The Hebrews cried out to God to save them from the oppressive Egyptians (Exodus 3:9). Samuel cried out to the Lord to save the Israelites from the hostile Philistines (1 Samuel 7:9). King Jehoshaphat cried to Jehovah when a vast army surrounded Jerusalem (2 Chronicles 20). Jonah cried out to God from the stomach of a whale (Jonah 2). Many of the psalms are simply the result of David and others repeatedly crying out to the Lord.

The person who comes passionately before God is crying out from the heart. It is the urgent appeal of the soul, looking and searching earnestly for God's presence. As far as I know the only requirement is that we are "righteous" before God. A righteous person is not a perfect person but one who has accepted Christ as Savior and has been imputed the righteousness of Jesus. "The righteous cry out, and the Lord hears them" (Psalm 34:17). As children of God, we have the inalienable right to bear our souls before our Father and pour out our hearts before him. We should follow the example of David: He poured out his "complaint" before the Lord (Psalm 142:2).

The heart cry of the desperate person isn't concerned about how his petition is worded or phrased. All that matters is an unburdening of the soul before God. It is after all the heart that God is most interested in, and the person who comes in heartfelt need is never turned away by our gracious Lord.

I think the most powerful element of sincere cries before the Savior is that in our humbled state we recognize that God is the only answer. When David was hiding in the cave from the terror of King Saul, he cried out to "God Most High, to God, who fulfills his purpose for me" (Psalm 57:2). Our only option is for God Almighty to act on our behalf. We have looked to others for help and found them wanting. We have tried our own resources and they have been insufficient. Unless God intervenes, we have no hope.

Praise God that he knows our frame and when we are weakest he is strongest. Our painful pleas come before his ears and he inclines his heart toward us. He gives us the mercy and grace we need to bear up under the load or to release us from the burden. The end of our rope is often the beginning of God's supernatural help. He waits for us to come to him with our heavy loads so that he may reveal himself to us as our great and awesome God.

Never be afraid to cry out to the Lord, to get down on your face or knees and let the tears flow and the pain come to the surface. He will answer you with his saving presence. He promises us that. "I waited patiently for the LORD; he turned to me and heard my cry" (Psalm 40:1).

———— ◦ ————

I know that you hear the cries of my heart, O God. Sometimes I am unable to put them into words, but even then you know the pain of my heart and meet me with lovingkindness. I am so grateful that you allow me to unburden my soul by coming to you in my distresses. Thank you that you never turn me away or tune me out.

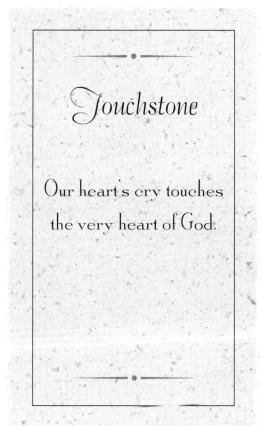

Touchstone

Our heart's cry touches
the very heart of God.

Do not be afraid. Stand firm and you will see the deliverance the LORD will bring you today.

EXODUS 14:13

Just Stand There

───── ⊛ ─────

When it comes to the list of Old Testament heroes, few have heard of Shammah. You find his name listed only once, but the mention is worthy.

Shammah was one of David's mighty men, a robust group of thirty comrades who fought alongside David and whose heroics were legendary. Within this group was an even more elite circle of three men. Shammah was one of the three. Here is why: "When the Philistines banded together at a place where there was a field full of lentils, Israel's troops fled from them. But Shammah took his stand in the middle of the field. He defended it and struck the Philistines down, and the Lord brought about a great victory" (2 Samuel 23:11–12).

The phrase "he stood his ground" has been a source of encouragement and inspiration for me because there are times in our lives when we are called on to take a stand. While others around us refuse to deal with the issue, the Lord speaks to our hearts that we need to stand firm and experience the real presence of Christ.

Sometimes, we need to hold our ground on key spiritual issues that are nonnegotiable. We need to wisely stand up for the clear absolutes of the Bible such as the inerrancy of Scripture and the deity of Christ. There can be no compromise here. When I served as president of my denomination, I was blessed to help lead them to reclaim these basic tenets. The road was hard, but God ultimately gave us victory.

There are times when we need to take a stand against personal sin in our lives. While the Lord graciously forgives us of our sins, we must never take it lightly. If we continue to indulge a certain sin, we run the risk of developing a hard heart toward God and others. There comes a time when we must deal ruthlessly with such sin, seeking genuine repentance. We may not experience instant victory—especially over a habitual sin—but God knows when we are serious, and he will give us the grace and power to live a righteous life. We are called to no longer be a slave of sin, but a pursuer of righteousness. A distaste for sin prepares our heart for a continual awareness of God's presence.

And there are distinct occasions when we need to take a bold stand against the Devil. Satan cannot alter our standing as God's sons and daughters, but he can make us miserable, harassing our emotions, infiltrating our thoughts. He is our enemy and we must take the authority of Christ over him. "Your enemy the devil prowls around like a roaring lion looking for someone to devour. Resist him, standing firm the faith" (1 Peter 5:8–9).

We must guard against undue pride, self-seeking motives, or overdependence on our flesh when we take resolute stands on such occasions. But we must not be afraid to do the right thing when God makes it clear that we are to follow him. He will give the victory that honors him.

———— ◆ ————

I do sense at times, Father, the need to stand firm in my faith. Help me to know how and when to trust you completely in these matters and bring me to a place of complete dependence on you. Search my heart and reveal to me my own errant ways that I may serve you in truth and purity. Give me the courageous faith to do the right thing.

Touchstone

You will never be let
down when you take
a firm stand on
God's promises.

I love the LORD, for he heard my voice.

PSALM 116:1

Prayer Works

will never forget the instance when I learned one of my most valuable lessons on prayer. I had taken a mission trip abroad to a rather remote country despite knowing about a crucial meeting that would take place in my absence. As I traveled from city to city, I found myself constantly worrying about the outcome of the meeting. I felt I had made the wrong decision, since I was sure that my presence at the deliberations was critical to its success. My mind was terribly distracted.

Although there was an eight-hour time difference, I decided to pray at the precise time the meeting was held. As I talked to the Lord in my hotel room late in the evening, God spoke clearly to my anxious spirit: "Charles, who would you rather attend the meeting, you or me?" I laughed out loud as God quickly put an end to my fretting and undue sense of importance.

I have never forgotten that moment and throughout my life prayer has been the most direct link to sense and experience God at work in my life. When we pray, we are entreating God to become involved in our circumstance and actively placing the results into his sovereign hand. Prayer brings God onto the scene, invoking his power, wisdom, and love.

What I needed at that moment, and what I continue to need daily, is to listen to what God has to say to me. Hearing God speak in the kind of conversational tone above doesn't happen frequently, but we can learn to keep our spiritual receptors attuned to God's wisdom. We begin by quieting our hearts and minds and being still before him. A busy, preoccupied mind has great difficulty in hearing the soft and gentle voice of the Savior.

I don't believe I would have heard the Lord speak directly to my need, had I not deliberately drawn aside.

The Lord speaks to our souls through the Scriptures. When we approach Scripture as listening to the voice of God, our time spent reading and studying will focus more on what God is saying to us. "What is this passage telling me?" "What should I do, Lord?" As a couple builds their relationship through conversation, we establish a personal relationship with the Father through our times in prayer with him. He delights in our dialogue with him because he wants us to know him and to reveal himself to us. He loves to hear his children talk with him.

The disciples asked Jesus to teach them one thing—how to pray (Luke 11:1). As they watched him retreat into the mountains and deserts to pray, they sensed that his power lay in his prayerful relationship with the Father. They rightly understood they needed to learn more about this spiritual dynamic.

We can too. Prayer is the supreme means by which we draw near to God to learn about him and his ways. It is great spiritual adventure and the surest way to invite him into our daily rounds.

———— ⚬ ————

Teach me, Lord, to call on you throughout the day—morning, noon, and evening—pouring out my heart to you in prayer. Thank you for being so near. You are eager to listen to my needs and even more eager to glorify your name through your answers. Lead me into rich fellowship with you as I come to you day by day.

Touchstone

You will never be
disappointed when
you call on God.

Let us not give up meeting together.

HEBREWS 10:25

The Body

The book of Acts is an incredible collection of the power of God. Miracles of healing, riveting sermons, amazing missionary journeys, great escapes, and a variety of other compelling deeds and events are recorded by Luke the physician. Yet, the centerpiece of that action-packed letter revolves around none other than the church of the Lord Jesus Christ.

Beginning with the second chapter on the day of Pentecost (the arrival of the Holy Spirit), the saga of the church unfolds as believers unite together. The church becomes the mainspring for the advancement of the gospel, and letters from the pens of apostles Paul, Peter, and John are primarily addressed to the churches that had been started throughout Asia Minor and Europe.

Little wonder then that our adversary, the Devil, will go to great lengths to damage the integrity and testimony of the church today. Dissension and divisions are almost the hallmark of the church, and few people have escaped at least some form of disagreement and disillusionment.

Despite the obvious flaws, the believer cannot survive the journey of faith apart from the ministry of the church. Gathered together, the church is still God's ordained place for the instruction and edification of the saints.

The writer of Hebrews urged the believers not to abandon the practice of regular worship together because the assembling of the church is where Christians are to find great encouragement. "Let us encourage one another—and all the more as you see the Day approaching" (Hebrews 10:25).

Through the study of Scripture and listening to the Word, believers find strength and hope. Through the worship of song and testimony, believers discover the wonder and transcendence of God. Through fellowship with one another, believers are comforted and supported. In every facet of assembly, the church is a place of spiritual and emotional encouragement for the saint.

God has so designed us that not only do we need him desperately, but we also need one another. I realize the latter equation can be difficult, but the church of the Lord Jesus Christ is one body made up of many members, each functioning for the glory of God and the blessing of each other.

We don't go to church completely out of duty, though obedience is essential. We assemble as one body in Christ because we are the living temple of the Holy Spirit, bound together to provide cheer and staying power for the race set before us. If you have distanced yourself from a local body, ask the Lord to lead you to a church where you can find the encouragement you need.

———— • ————

Father, thank you for creating the church. In your wisdom and love, you knew I would need the fellowship of other believers to help me experience the reality of your presence. Help me to see the church as a place where I receive and give encouragement. Thank you that you made us to fellowship with one another. Forgive me for the times when I am reluctant to become involved and, by your grace, place me into the local body where you are gloriously present.

Touchstone

God's presence is
readily enjoyed in the
company of other
believers.

For God was pleased to have all his fullness dwell in him ... making peace through his blood, shed on the cross.

COLOSSIANS 1:19–20

The Reconciling Cross

---

here is only one explanation why the people of God can experience his abiding, eternal presence and that is the cross of Jesus Christ. The cross is the wisdom and power of God (1 Corinthians 1:24) that has rescued sinful man to right relationship with Holy God and made possible every benefit of a personal relationship with the Savior.

Only the cross of Jesus Christ could bridge the vast gap between God and man. "But now in Christ Jesus you who once were far away have been brought near through the blood of Christ" (Ephesians 2:13). The blood of Christ speaks of his sacrificial death where he bore the sin of man. Peter writes similarly that "Christ died for sins once for all, the righteous for the unrighteous, to bring you to God" (1 Peter 3:18). Unless God had taken the initiative to send Christ to earth and the cross, he could not possibly extend the offer of his personal presence to men and women. The cross brings us near to God and his enduring friendship and fellowship.

The cross of Christ is what reconciles us to God who has "reconciled us to himself through Christ and gave us the ministry of reconciliation: that God was reconciling the world to himself in Christ, not counting men's sins against them" (2 Corinthians 5:18–19). Estranged by our sinful nature, we find a just and lasting peace with the Lord through his cross. There God became sin for us that we might become the righteousness of God in Christ. There God died in our stead that we might receive everlasting life.

The cross of Christ is where we were justified by God. Our sins deserved a just judgment. Christ on the cross bore the wrath of God that we might be forgiven. He placed his only begotten Son on the tree of Calvary "so as to be just and the one who justifies those who have faith in Jesus" (Romans 3:26). The cross is just as much an expression of the justice of God as it is his love. It is as one scholar said, the holy love of God for men. God could not overlook sin. It must be dealt with, and it was in the person of his son on the cross once and for all.

The cross of Christ is where we were redeemed from our life of sin and death. "In him, we have redemption through his blood, the forgiveness of sins" (Ephesians 1:7). The death of Jesus Christ on the cross was the ransom he paid to free us from our bondage to sin. It cost the Father the death of his son to liberate us, to purchase us from our old, futile way of living. There is nothing cheap about grace.

The cross of Christ is where sin, death, the law, and the Devil were defeated. The hour of Christ's death was the consummate triumph of eternity where all of our foes were routed by our Savior. We triumph over these enemies because we share in the triumph of Christ Jesus over them.

Christ's cross has made it possible for all men to draw near and stay near to the Savior. The only criterion is that we place our faith in his substitutionary, sacrificial, all-sufficient, atoning death. When we do, we are forever in the presence of the Savior and forever in the shadow of the cross.

———— ✦ ————

Thank you, my Savior, that you brought me to the Father through your atoning death on the cross. Thank you that I enjoy all the fruits of a righteous life through your death for my sin. Help me keep your cross and your resurrection life in the center of my thinking that I may always cherish the foundation of my relationship with you.

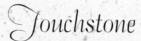

Touchstone

The shadow of the
Almighty is the shadow
of Christ's cross.

Has God forgotten to be merciful?

PSALM 77:9

Silent But Never Still

⸺ ◉ ⸺

*N*oah had been in the ark for almost five long months. The rains had come for forty days and nights, and the wait for the water to recede must have seemed interminable. Sure, God had saved Noah and his family from the flood, but how long would Noah, his family, and a cargo full of restless animals have to wait? Have you ever spent five months on a boat?

"But God remembered Noah" (Genesis 8:1). Much to his relief, God remained faithful to his promise and placed Noah and his crew on dry ground in the remaining months. Had God forgotten Noah? No. An omniscient God forgets nothing, especially when it comes to the plight of his people. The term "remembrance" is used by the human authors of Scripture to describe God's activity after a seeming lapse of involvement.

However, surviving those difficult days when it appears that our cries for help have been ignored can be a stern challenge for our faith. Prayers seemingly go unanswered. Circumstances go from bad to worse. The pressure mounts.

Remember this: God may be silent, but he is never still. God is always at work in your life to bring about his purpose and plan. "For it is God who works in you to will and to act according to his good purpose" (Philippians 2:13). You can count on this, regardless of the circumstances. There is never a time when an omnipresent God is not constantly, unceasingly active in your life for your eventual good and his glory.

Remember this: God will never abandon you. "Never will I leave you; never will I forsake you" (Hebrews 13:5). The Lord is our constant companion. He is not a fair-weathered friend, and he has pledged his covenant love to us for eternity. We simply can't let our unreliable feelings overshadow the reality of God's commitment to our welfare, demonstrated once and for all through the sacrifice of Christ for our sins.

Remember this: God is always on the scene. "Surely I am with you always, to the very end of the age" (Matthew 28:20). This is the kind of God that we can trust without reservation, that we can depend on in any kind of storm.

The prophet Isaiah wrote in response to Israel's cry that God had apparently forgotten her: "Can a mother forget the baby at her breast and have no compassion on the child she has borne? Though she may forget, I will not forget you! See, I have engraved you on the palms of my hands" (Isaiah 49:15–16).

You are always on God's mind. He has gripped us for eternity. Always keep that in your mind.

———— • ————

There are times when I wonder where you are, Father. It seems that you are a long way off, but I know deep in my heart that you are always with me and for me. Help me to keep a steady gaze on your faithfulness when my doubts and questions arise, for I know that you will never abandon me. There is no one like you.

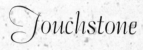

Touchstone

We may forget God, but
he never forgets us.

If you love me, you will obey what I command. And I will ask the Father, and he will give you another Counselor to be with you forever—the Spirit of truth.

JOHN 14:15–17

The Blessings of the Trinity

$\mathcal{E}$xperiencing the presence of God for the Christian is always an encounter with the Trinity. Although the word *trinity* does not occur in Scripture, God is defined as a triune deity who exists in the person of the Father, the Son, and the Holy Spirit. God is one in essence, but there are three distinct persons, all being God. The Father is God (1 Corinthians 8:6); the Son, Jesus Christ, is God (Hebrews 1:8–10); and the Holy Spirit is God (Acts 5:3–4).

The Trinity is not a sterile doctrine. The persons of the Father, the Son, and the Holy Spirit are in a distinctly special relationship with each believer, each with a special sense of communicating the glorious presence of the Godhead. With the excruciating cross only a few hours away, Jesus spent his last hours talking to his disciples about the persons of the Trinity. Joyously, we have the privilege of knowing our God in relationship with the three persons of the Trinity.

We have fellowship with God the Father. The One who has sent Jesus and the Spirit to secure and apply redemption is the One we can know in an intimate fashion. He is our "Abba, Father" (Romans 8:15) and we are his children. Jesus spoke of God the Father more than forty times in the Upper Room Discourse (John 13–17), helping his disciples understand the Father's love for them. After his resurrection, Christ told them he would return to "my Father and your Father, to my God and your God" (John 20:17).

We have fellowship with God the Son, Jesus, our Savior and Lord. "And our fellowship is with the Father and with his Son, Jesus Christ" (1 John 1:3). Jesus is our kinsman-redeemer to whom we can go with our burdens, complaints, and joys. He is our Friend with whom we share our deepest longings. He is our elder Brother who has become like us that he might become our gracious High Priest (Hebrews 2:11–18).

We have fellowship with God the Holy Spirit. He is our divine paraclete, the One called alongside to help. He indwells our spirits, making Christ and his glory known and illuminating the Scriptures that we might know the Father and the Son. He is our divine Guide, Advocate, and Teacher.

The richness of the orthodox Christian faith lies in our glorious relationship with a triune God who manifests his presence in the splendor of each glorious person of the Godhead. "May the grace of the Lord Jesus Christ, and the love of God, and the fellowship of the Holy Spirit be with you all" (2 Corinthians 13:14). The fullness and richness of relationship with God is with the Father, the Son, and the Spirit.

———— ◆ ————

I come to you, O God, in worship and adoration. I thank you that you are one God who exists in the persons of the Father, the Son, and the Spirit. You are perfect in unity. I am so blessed to know you. Lead me into deeper relationship with yourself as you reveal the glories of your Personhood.

Touchstone

We are in fellowship
with God the Father,
God the Son, and
God the Spirit.

Turn to me and be gracious to me, for I am lonely and afflicted.

PSALM 25:16

Never Alone

———— ❖ ————

*L*oneliness is one of the most crushing human emotions. The feelings of abandonment and isolation create an overwhelming sense of helplessness and despair. People in the throes of a heightened state of loneliness often fall prey to temptations or behaviors that are extremely atypical. It is a dangerous place to be.

Jesus knows what it is like to be lonely. As the perfect Son of God, he certainly was unlike all the other children in Nazareth. And we all know when a person is different from the crowd, they usually spend time by themselves. Shortly after he began his public ministry, many of the disciples left him when his teachings became too difficult to grasp. At the time of his greatest sorrow, the handful that remained scattered, leaving him utterly alone.

As our sympathetic High Priest who "had to be made like his brothers in every way" (Hebrews 2:17) and who "shared in [our] humanity" (Hebrews 2:14), Jesus is intimately acquainted with the devastating effect of loneliness. He is also able to come to our aid with help and hope that can lift us out of the deepest pit.

Jesus hears our heart cry. The faintest whisper of a heart that feels alone and abandoned comes before the heart of a loving Father who will go to any lengths to comfort his children. In fact, he has already gone to the extreme in offering himself for us on the cross and since he did not spare his only son, he will freely give us the help we need (Romans 8:32). When Hagar and her son were dying in the desert after being cast out by Sarah, God heard her feeble voice and nurtured them. When Elijah sat alone after his power encounter with the prophets of Baal, he sat down and collapsed, wondering if he was the only one left in Israel who still called on God. The Lord encouraged him with the news of many others, though he knew none of them.

Throughout the Scriptures when men and women of faith faced great challenges, God reminded them of his powerful presence, saying to them, "I am with you." They were afraid, anxious, doubtful, and bewildered, but the awareness of God's presence became their strength to deal with formidable odds. Lonely leaders were instilled with courage, lonely prophets with boldness, lonely apostles with hope.

Remember, *God* is with us. The God who is able. The God who is kind. The God who is merciful. The God who is gentle. The God who knows all our needs. The God who is faithful. The God who works all things together for good. The God who loves us with an everlasting love.

God has already turned to you through the indwelling presence of his Spirit. His face shines upon you. Turn to him and find the solace and help you need. It may come through a Scripture promise. It may come through a prayer. It may come through his still voice when you are quiet on your bed. But it will come, because he has come into your life forever.

———— ◦ ————

Jesus, you do know what loneliness is like. You understand when I come to you with my feelings and do not condemn me. Thank you for allowing me to express my inner pain to you. You are always there for me and you will never cast me out. I run into your arms.

Touchstone

God has turned to you so
that you might turn to him.

And we know that in all things God works for the good
of those who love him, who have been called according to his purpose.

ROMANS 8:28

No Second Causes

While there are numerous mileposts on the road to a mature faith, there is one fundamental truth that can help us make increasing strides to a spiritually sound and solid Christianity. This principle is especially true as we encounter roadblocks and adversities that often can take us backwards in our faith.

Here is the biblical paradigm: There are no second causes in the life of the believer. This means that God himself is ultimately behind everything that happens to us. What a difficult notion to accept, particularly in our setbacks, but what a sure foundation for a steadfast faith. The better we come to understand this, the greater progress and peace we will experience in our relationship with Christ.

Think about Joseph. Raised in an affluent home, he was sold into slavery as a teenager by jealous and angry brothers. He spent at least the next ten years in servitude in Pharaoh's house and, worse, in an Egyptian jail. Only after those many painful years did the Lord deliver him and make him second in charge in the most powerful nation on earth.

How did Joseph survive those cruel years? Listen to his words in the final chapter of Genesis as he tells his brothers of God's role in his incredible story. "You intended to harm me, but God intended it for good to accomplish what is now being done, the saving of many lives" (Genesis 50:20).

Behind it all—the treachery, the betrayal, the imprisonment—Joseph saw God at work. The brothers did indeed commit "evil" against him. Their wickedness caused real pain and suffering. Joseph never denied this. But what he affirmed over and above the evil was his sovereign God at work. Such is the greatness and absolute reign of Christ, that he works even through the harmful motives and acts of men to accomplish his purpose and plan for our lives. When evil touches our lives or the lives of those we love, God has allowed it. He is never the author of evil, but he directs it for his own sovereign and good purposes.

Spiritually mature Christians, through God's grace and counsel, develop a spiritual perspective that sees the hand of God in full control of our lives and the circumstances that touch them. They bow before the Lord in submission, with the full comprehension that an all-knowing, all-wise, all-powerful God is working through both good and bad events to produce the character of Christ.

Jerry Bridges writes in *Trusting God*, "Over all the actions and events of our lives, God is in control doing as He pleases, not apart from these events, or in spite of them, but *through* them."

Joseph saw through the hands of his brothers to the hand of God.

Your times are squarely in God's hands, not anyone else's. He works all things together for your good as you submit to his loving sovereignty.

———— • ————

Help me to see your hand at work in all the events of my life, Lord, good and bad. Enable me to respond to my circumstances with the knowledge that you are in control, so I need not fear or panic. Grant me the growing maturity to trust you absolutely in any and every circumstance.

Touchstone

We can give thanks
to God in all things
because God is in
control of all things.

Hide me in the shadow of your wings.

PSALM 17:8

In The Shadow

---

*S*ince the Advent of Christ and the gift of the Holy Spirit were still in the future, the writers of the Old Testament searched for language that expressed the nearness of God. Terms of endearment such as having our names inscribed on God's palms were employed, but there is one word picture that the writers used on several occasions—*shadow*.

As the shadow of a man represented his likeness and proximity, so the shadow of God intimated the moral and spiritual presence of the living God among his people. "He who dwells in the shelter of the Most High will rest in the shadow of the Almighty," wrote the psalmist (Psalm 91:1).

Not only did "shadow" suggest the eminence of the Lord, it also helped the readers make an instant connection with the character and purpose of his presence. In a region of burning heat, sand, and rocks, a shadow was a place of enormous comfort.

Dwelling in the shadow of God was and is a place of protection. The Hebrew word for *Almighty* is *Shaddai*, an appellation that connotes the power of God for our personal protection from evil. The person who lives near God is one who knows how to resist the Devil and his enticements to sin because he clearly understands that God himself is the one who shields him from the power of the adversary. Every day, we face battles far beyond our capabilities. We are no match for the forces of evil. We must cling to the Lord and count on his safekeeping.

The shadow of the Lord is likewise a place of rest and refuge. We are easily bothered and heated over the upsets that life brings.

Unless we learn to look to the Lord for soul rest, we will find our energy sapped and our joy zapped. God's character—his love, peace, faithfulness—are the perfect resting places for the believer. Resting in God's love and provision, we can renew our spirits and our bodies. Rather than continue to fight, there are times when we simply need to rest in the Lord. Finding our refuge in God is just as significant. The Hebrew words for *refuge* and *faith* are closely related. The constant urging to take refuge in God is but another way to encourage us to place our trust in him. God wants to be trusted and when we do so, we discover his sufficiency for our needs.

Dwelling in God's shadow brings great reassurance as well. God does love us and care for us, even when we think he may not. He is there, for us and with us, overshadowing us with his presence. "I have . . . covered you with the shadow of my hand" (Isaiah 51:16).

———— ✦ ————

I need to sense the comfort of your refreshing presence, Lord. May you renew my spirit and ease my tensions as I come to take refuge in you and find my rest in your character. Teach me to come to you daily, so that I may not become so wearied and worn.

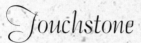

Touchstone

He is with us and for us,
overshadowing us with
his presence.

Rejoice that your names are written in heaven.

LUKE 10:20

Terms of Endearment

God's presence in our lives is always defined in intimate fashion. Jesus loved the disciples. They loved him. Jesus spent time in the homes of people like Martha and Mary, dining with them, laughing with them. Not only are we servants of the Most High God, we are also his friends.

This intimacy is revealed in several relational metaphors: Jesus is the shepherd, we are the sheep. As the shepherd cares for and protects the sheep, we are constantly provided for by the Savior. The Lord God is our father, we are his children, kept safely in his love.

Beyond the metaphors is even more descriptive language that unveils the heart of God for his people. He sees and remembers our tears. "Record my lament; list my tears on your scroll— are they not in your record?" (Psalm 56:8). Tears—of joy or sorrow—are some of the deepest expression of our being. God sees and notes each droplet and one day promises to wipe them away. What other god of any religion or creed knows the tracks of our tears and keeps them in his memory? The lonely cry of a heart on a bed at night, the sudden outburst of a child, the ache of the elderly in a nursing home—all of these touch the heart of God.

God knows our names. When you speak with someone you know or love, you call them by their name. Our names carry an integral part of our being. In the Hebrew culture, names were particularly meaningful, signifying a specific character trait or marking a poignant experience. God calls us and deals with us by name, not en masse, but individually. Saul heard God call out his name as he traveled on the Damascus road. The disciples heard Jesus address them by their names.

"He calls his own sheep by name and leads them out" (John 10:3). God knows and understands Charles Stanley. He speaks to me, in my innermost being in the most personal manner. I recall several occasions when the Lord whispered my name as I sought him: "Charles, you know how much I love you." Hearing the Lord speak my name in my spirit brought an amazing calm and fresh awareness of his presence. Listen quietly and attentively and you will hear the Lord speak your name as well.

Again, I say that no other faith on earth can speak of a God such as Jehovah who so lovingly and tenderly deals with his people. Their gods are stern and forbearing, distant and unapproachable, with no hint of intimacy. But our Father in heaven, creator of mankind, stars, heavens, and galaxies, has chosen to reveal his presence to us through his Word and his son in the most affectionate way. This is why we have a personal relationship with the Father, the Son, and the Spirit, and he deals personally with each of us.

What a Savior!

———— ◆ ————

Thank you, Jesus, that I know your name and that you know mine. You speak to me just as personably as you did with your disciples when you were on earth. Even the stars have a name that you have given them. Help me to hear your voice and follow you, to listen to the Spirit as he guides and directs me.

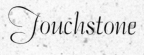Touchstone

Our personal God
relates to us the most
personal of ways.

He rescued me because he delighted in me.

PSALM 18:19

The Divine Pursuer

—————— ⬤ ——————

In the movie *Driving Miss Daisy* the widow's chauffeur has an opportunity to drive for another affluent lady in town. He discusses his options with Miss Daisy's son and is offered a nice salary increase along with a number of compliments. Exiting the office, he remarks with a wry smile that "it sure is nice to be wanted."

We all like to feel wanted. Think how you felt when someone extended you a job, when a coach picked you for the team, when friends invited you to join them for a trip. That sense of being someone special is vital to a proper sense of well-being.

One of the most remarkable aspects of the Christian faith is that God is divinely pursuing us. He isn't passively sitting in the heavens waiting for judgment day on poor souls who haven't been given a clue to his existence. He has acted decisively in history to reveal himself and his ways and to demonstrate his passion to rescue his people.

The entire narrative of Scripture, spanning thousands of years and three continents, is the spellbinding story of God's relentless pursuit of relationship. We exist because it was the Godhead's idea to make man and woman in his very own image. We are redeemed from the bondage of sin because God worked unceasingly to provide salvation through the incarnation, life, death, burial, and resurrection of his son, Jesus Christ. We experience the reality of his personal presence and power through the indwelling of the Holy Spirit.

This steadfast love flows from God's desire to revel in his people so that he might be glorified. He doesn't just tolerate us;

he rejoices in us. "The LORD your God is with you, he is mighty to save. He will take great delight in you, he will quiet you with his love, he will rejoice over you with singing" (Zephaniah 3:17). This doesn't sound like a God who has methodically gone about the work of creation and redemption does it? It is the heartbeat of a God who delights in his people.

We are not brought into fellowship with Christ through our personal efforts; we come by faith through the active wooing of the Spirit of God. He has chosen us to be with him forever. "For he chose us in him before the creation of the world to be holy and blameless in his sight" (Ephesians 1:4). God's gracious activity on our behalf makes our faith possible. It isn't that he needs us; the Lord needs nothing for his completeness. He has *chosen* to need us.

In a culture dominated by greed and power, alienation and discouragement are potent predators of the soul. We triumph as we see God as the great lover of our souls. No sin can turn him away. No failure can thwart his pursuit of our welfare. He pursues us today and every day with his great love. Others may ignore or reject us, but God our Father has accepted us for eternity and given us all we need for life and godliness. What more could we ask?

———— • ————

To think that you wanted to save me because you chose to do so thrills me. I praise you, Father, that you are not methodically counting down to a severe day of judgment but that you are pursuing the salvation and joy for as many who would put their faith in your son. Thank you that I am worthy because you have set your love upon me.

Touchstone

God has chosen you
to be part of his family
and actively seeks your
good and his glory.

Blessed is the man who perseveres under trial.

JAMES 1:12

Draw Near in Adversity

dversity is something we naturally shrink from. Obstacles and trials are by their nature intrinsically unpleasant. The more severe the adversity, the more our bodies and emotions are drained by the demands. The longer the problem continues, the more difficult it becomes to maintain our stamina and perspective.

Yet the Bible is certainly clear about one thing—adversity is used by God in exponentially powerful ways to develop our character and confidence in him. When suffering and pain rock our world, we can find comfort and strength in the sure knowledge that the Lord is using our struggles to draw us near to him.

The Lord uses our adversities to hone our faith. There is no easy believism in times of testing. Simple answers and simple solutions are discarded and the reality of our trust in God is exposed. Will we still trust him even when the events that have precipitated our troubles are unexplainable? Job, a righteous man of his time, lost his family and possessions in one traumatic event. Though he wrestled with his tremendous loss, he still confessed that "though he slay me, yet will I hope in him" (Job 13:15). Peter, who knew his share of pain, wrote that adversity hammers on our lives so that our faith "may be proved genuine" (1 Peter 1:7).

The Lord uses our adversities to cultivate our personal devotion. Personal devotion to Christ in time of ease is good; personal devotion to Christ in time of suffering is better. God is looking for men and women who are personally devoted to him, whose hearts are loyal to him. One description of the Hebrews who turned away from following God is that their "hearts were not loyal to God, [their] spirits were not faithful to him" (Psalm 78:8). Followers or disciples of Christ will inevitably face seasons in life when their allegiance to him will be tested.

The Lord uses our adversities to develop the indispensable trait of perseverance. James said that we should actually welcome our trials because "you know that the testing of your faith develops perseverance" and perseverance helps us to be "mature and complete" (James 1:3–4). The ability to stay on course in our walk with Christ allows us to bring a mature, godly faith to our troubles and prepares us to comfort others who experience similar difficulties.

There are no shortcuts to a genuine, robust faith. The strong winds of adversity that rage against us can work to our advantage as we see Christ come through for us again and again. The pain is real. The heartache and disappointment are real. But so is our confidence in God. The trouble actually brings us closer to him. The suffering brings us to greater dependence on him.

Don't run away from your pain. Don't blame God. Don't abandon the faith that has sustained you through the years. These are real temptations, but the consequences of yielding are still more painful. Draw near to God in your trial and you have his promise that he will draw near to you.

———— • ————

I come to draw near to you, Lord. I have been battered by this adversity for some time now and have come close to slipping. But I still want to trust you and realize that I must continually throw my burdens upon you. Thank you for your love and comfort in the midst of my trials and that you will use my suffering to deepen my relationship with you.

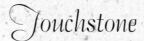

Touchstone

Our faith is tested that
it might grow stronger.

When I was in great need, he saved me.

PSALM 116:6

Present in Need

---◆---

In time of distress or demand, the human body is an amazing creation. For example, when a person runs for a long distance, the body pumps an extra supply of blood to the lower extremities. When the skin is cut, platelets rush to the wound to stop the flow of blood. When an infection attacks a certain part of the body, antibodies scramble to the site of the contagion. The paradigm is that help and healing move to the point of need.

There is a close parallel in the spiritual life. God's blessings and help flow to those who stand in most need. The self-reliant person, oblivious to his need for Christ and the Spirit, rarely partakes of abundant and eternal life. His hubris and self-sufficiency blind him to his poverty of soul and spirit. He has no need for God, and thus no part in him.

But God's help and succor surge toward the needy. When Hannah poured out her soul to the Lord in her anguish over childlessness, God answered with a son, Samuel, and Hannah's prayer to the Lord praises him who "raises the poor from the dust and lifts the needy from the ash heap" (1 Samuel 2:8). Our need, whatever it may be, is the signal for God's great supply, for it is our "needs" that God richly supplies with his superabundant provision (Philippians 4:19).

Our need forces us to admit our inadequacies. They peel away our layers of arrogance and independence, exposing our true weaknesses and frailties. But in God's great paradox, our poverty is precisely the right spiritual primer for his riches. To the weak and needy, God sends his power. Paul exclaimed, "Therefore, I will boast all the more gladly about my weaknesses, so that Christ's power may rest on me. That is why, for Christ's sake, I delight in weaknesses. . . . For when I am weak, then I am strong" (2 Corinthians 12:9–10).

There is no shortfall of God's gracious help and blessing. His inexhaustible supply is tapped, however, by the weak, the wounded, the weary. The mercy of God runs strong toward those who have made a mess of things; the forgiveness of God swiftly flows toward those who have sinned; the peace of Christ courses toward those who are troubled and anxious. Jesus ministered to those who knew their poverty—Mary Magdalene, the Samaritan woman, the lepers, the blind—not the self-righteous Pharisees and Sadducees.

Never feel guilty because you have great needs. Never feel you can't come to Christ because you have been brought low by your own sin or by circumstances. This is exactly the right time to come before the Savior who welcomes all those who come to his loving presence. We can come before the throne of grace with great confidence and assurance and receive mercy and grace in "our time of need" (Hebrews 4:16).

———— • ————

My needs are great, Lord. I sometimes try and hide them from you but that only makes things worse. You know my heart anyway. I bring them to you knowing that your help and comfort run swiftly to my point of need. Thank you that you have made me that I might need you and that you are the ever-gracious Savior who never turns me away.

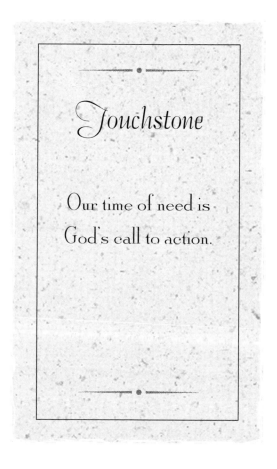

Touchstone

Our time of need is
God's call to action.

He is my God, and I will praise him.

EXODUS 15:2

Worthy Is the Lord

here is something about praising God that brings his presence into the midst of our circumstances in a vivid way.

When King Jehoshaphat faced an overwhelming opposing army, he sent his singer out to battle with the war cry of "Give thanks to the Lord, for his love endures forever" (2 Chronicles 20:21). A rout ensued. When the apostle Paul and his companion, Silas, were tossed into a Philippian jail, they worshiped God and their chains were broken when an earthquake rocked the jail.

I haven't experienced that kind of drama, but learning to praise God in the heat of the fray is one spiritual exercise that has focused my attention on God's very real presence. Hundreds, if not thousands of times, by God's grace, I have turned to God in worship when my circumstances were ominous. I am always encouraged and strengthened.

God delights in our praise because we ascribe to him his true worth. He is the most magnificent being we can conceive of. In the book of Revelation, angels and men are constantly bowing at his feet and declaring the wonder of the Redeemer (Revelation 4:9–11). Such praise rivets our emotions and thoughts on the greatness of God, which in turns brings our troubles into manageable perspective. What relationship can God not heal? What obstacle can God not remove? What fear can God not banish? The more we praise, the more we magnify God's delivering presence.

Our praise honors God because it is evidence of our trust in him. The writer of Hebrews speaks of a "sacrifice of praise—the fruit of lips that confess his name" (Hebrews 13:15). Coming before the Lord and confessing his faithfulness and love in time of trouble is the most genuine expression of confident faith I know. We abandon ourselves to trusting God by cultivating a heart of praise in adversity. We tell him, and he loves to hear it, that we are quietly and expectantly waiting on his answer.

God is always at the center of the universe. Worshipful people place God at the center of their lives. They enthrone the majestic Christ in the seat of all personal experiences. They learn to think rightly and highly about God. "It is fitting for the upright to praise him," said the psalmist, and I have yet to find the occasion when that was not true (Psalm 33:1).

Go to the Lord in praise when your soul is cold and the night is dark. It may be a struggle to start, but find a verse that describes God's goodness and greatness and pray that Scripture to the Lord. Don't expect your emotions to instantly register a sense of God's presence, but continue to fix your heart on praising him, and watch for the sure and steady influx of his strength and hope. You have rightly exalted God and he will exalt you in due time.

———— ◆ ————

I come to you in worship today, most gracious Father. You are more than worthy of the praise that I can give, and I do so with my whole heart. Help me to see your true worth so that I may know you rightly and trust you unreservedly. I enter into your presence with thanksgiving and adoration and entrust myself to you. You will withhold no good thing from me, and for this, I am grateful.

Touchstone

Worship enthrones God
at the center of my life.

"Do not I fill heaven and earth?" declares the LORD.

JEREMIAH 23:24

Our Ever-Present Help

A well-known European physician had this inscription engraved over the door of his house: "Bidden or not bidden, God is here." These words are a pithy reminder of the omnipresence of God. God, in his completeness, fills all space in heaven, earth, and beyond and yet is never limited by it. As one theologian put it, "God, in the totality of his essence, without diffusion or expansion, multiplication or division, penetrates and fills the universe in all its parts."

David was in awe of such a God. "Where can I go from your Spirit? Where can I flee from your presence? If I go up to the heavens, you are there; if I make my bed in the depths, you are there. If I rise on the wings of the dawn, if I settle on the far side of the sea, even there your hand will guide me, your right hand will hold me fast" (Psalm 139:7–10). Wherever David could go, God was already there.

The reality that we cannot escape from the presence of the living God is a disturbing thought for the unbeliever. "Everything is uncovered and laid bare before the eyes of him to whom we must give account" (Hebrews 4:13). One cannot run or hide from a God who is everywhere. But for the disciple of Christ, the verity of God's all-encompassing presence is a tremendous comfort.

God was there with Moses in the suffocating heat of the desert. God was there when David hid in caves and clefts. God was there when Daniel was thrust into the lions' den. God was there when Nehemiah rebuilt the charred walls of Jerusalem. God was there when Paul and Silas were bloodied and bruised in a Philippian jail. God was there when John was exiled to an Aegean island.

Perhaps that is what moved David to declare that God was his "ever-present help in trouble" (Psalm 46:1). An omnipresent God is abundantly available to come to our rescue. He is always near to us (Psalm 145:18). He is always there to strengthen, redeem, pardon, encourage, guide, and bless us.

This should bring us great joy. "You will fill me with joy in your presence, with eternal pleasures at your right hand" (Psalm 16:11). Joy is always possible with our Lord who is always with us. He cannot abandon or forsake us because he is always there. This is the kind of God we can trust. This is the kind of God we can worship.

———— • ————

I find great comfort in knowing that you are my ever-present help. Lord. I really do not face anything alone. You are with me always. Let me run quickly to you when I face trouble or danger and continually fill my heart with the keen sense of your living. active presence.

Touchstone

Joy is always possible
with the God who
is always there.

Trust in the LORD with all your heart and lean not on your own understanding.

PROVERBS 3:5

Perplexity Is Okay

---

*O*ne of the most difficult tensions in the Christian journey is the balance between expectations and reality. One of the biggest gaps that I have encountered in my fifty years as a believer is what I call the perplexity factor.

For whatever reason, I have found that most Christians, including myself, who receive Christ believe we have tapped into a storehouse of wisdom and knowledge that will unlock all the mysteries of life. Indeed, believers do enter into an extraordinary relationship with an omniscient God, but our treasure is still contained in a finite vessel. God can see around the bend, but we can't.

Here's the bottom line: God has it all figured out, but we don't. Paul put it this way when he addressed the Corinthians: "We are . . . perplexed, but not in despair" (2 Corinthians 4:8). Even the great apostle admitted that he couldn't quite understand everything that had happened to him. They left him somewhat bewildered and confused, but never emotionally distraught. Just because he couldn't fathom all of God's dealings didn't mean he was defeated or downcast. St. Augustine was said to have commented on one troubling verse of Scripture with, "Meaning of this scripture completely escapes me."

What I have discovered is that perplexity is pretty much a normal state for the Christian. We serve an infinite God who is always working to bring about his agenda, but we are not privy to the schedule or the means to accomplish it. His ways and thoughts are completely different than ours (Isaiah 55:8), so finding ourselves perplexed over the turns and seasons of the

Christian experience should be expected. We are bound to face events and circumstances that challenge our preconceived notions and raise questions.

That's okay. Our state of puzzlement is exactly where our trust in Christ is shaped and molded. The righteous, after all, do live by faith, and that trust is galvanized when the reality of our predicaments a far cry from our expectations. The place of perplexity is a call for renewed confidence in the sovereign love of God, who is orchestrating all things for his glory and our good.

Our quandaries are in reality a time of testing for our faith. Obedience to God's clear commands is one thing, but trusting God when few things make sense is still another. Muscular Christians are built in these trying seasons.

Actually, accepting perplexity as an ordinary state in our faith walk can be liberating. I remember the days when I thought I had to have the answer for everyone's problems. I agonized over just the right thing to say, worrying that somehow I had to defend God's position. Thankfully, the Lord delivered me from such presumptuousness, helping me realize that he is the only one who knows the end from the beginning.

If you are perplexed over circumstances, relax in God's care for you. He may soon show you the way out, or he may not. What is important is not what you know, but Whom you know. He will bring you through.

I find myself thinking that I must know all the answers, Lord, and what a frustrating exercise that is. Release me from the bondage of trying to understand it all and give me the grace I need to simply trust you in my perplexity. I know that you care for me and that is enough.

Touchstone

It is not what you know
that is critical, but
Whom you know.

But thanks be to God, who ... through us spreads
everywhere the fragrance of the knowledge of him.

2 CORINTHIANS 2:14

The Fragrance of Christ

'll never forget the prayer a young man prayed as we talked about his upcoming mission trip to a Central Asian country. He had some of the normal anxieties and a tremendous amount of enthusiasm. But it was this statement that arrested me: "Lord, I pray that those who encounter me during my stay also encounter you."

That struck me in a profound manner. He wanted the contact between him and others to be a genuine encounter with the person of Christ himself. I wonder what would happen if each of us adopted that same thought. How would our days be different if each morning we asked Christ to so permeate our words and deeds that others would sense the reality of Christ's indwelling presence?

The presence of Christ is to be radiated to those around us—our families, coworkers, friends, acquaintances, even our enemies. We can't keep the gospel a secret. Christ, who has come to inhabit our soul through the Holy Spirit, affects our behavior so others can see and hear the changes he works within us.

I remember a certain professor at the seminary I attended. Whenever he taught, I listened attentively because his actions and demeanor vividly communicated the presence of the living Christ. The occasions I had to visit with him in his study were all memorable. He was so godly in everything that he said and did that I always came away with an almost palpable sense of having been in the presence of Christ.

The apostle Paul wrote, "I have been crucified with Christ and I no longer live, but Christ lives in me. The life I live in the body, I live by faith in the Son of God, who loved me and gave himself for me" (Galatians 2:20). In almost every book he authored, Paul spoke of the new man that he had become through the sacrificial death, burial, and resurrection of Jesus Christ. The old Paul had been crucified with the Savior and the new Paul was now alive through the indwelling presence of Christ. Jesus had come to take up residence in Paul, the truth that Paul often expressed as "Christ in you" (Colossians 1:27). It was the core of Paul's theology and is the center of our new existence in Christ.

I think this is pivotal if we are to grasp the great adventure that awaits us as followers of Christ. We can communicate the presence of the Savior because it is the Lord himself who lives within. The people we come into daily contact with can experience an encounter with Christ as we submit to his lordship.

Christ lives within, not simply to change us, but to give solid evidence of his magnificent presence. Will we let him have his way with us that we may show others the Way?

———— • ————

Lord, so fill me with your resurrection life today that my speech and conduct may reflect your presence. I want my relationships with others to be opportunities for encounters with you. Let them see you at work in my life. Especially take the rough corners of my personality and shape them into your likeness. Thank you for the privilege of sharing your life with so many who need hope and encouragement.

Touchstone

May those who
encounter me today
encounter you as well.

Live a life worthy of the calling you have received.

EPHESIANS 4:1

Get Serious

*I*t is amazing how quickly our attitude and behavior can change when we get serious. A stern warning from our doctor rivets our attention. An alarming call from a wayward son or daughter brings us to our knees. We become all business and direct all of our energies toward a solution.

God expects us to take him seriously. His word to a wavering King Asa was, "For the eyes of the LORD range throughout the earth to strengthen those whose hearts are fully committed to him" (2 Chronicles 16:9). In other words, God is intensely looking for those people who are bold enough to earnestly trust him.

The believer in Jesus Christ should be completely serious about the holiness of God. The Lord God is a holy God. Peter tells us that because God is holy, "so be holy in all you do" (1 Peter 1:15). The person who is serious about the holiness of God is far more likely to experience the powerful presence of Christ in conduct and conversation. Growth in holiness means that we become more like Jesus and this continual transformation of mind and spirit is the most exciting adventure I know.

The believer in Jesus Christ should be completely serious about sin. Sin was serious enough to God that he sent his son to die on a cross in our place. Sin brought death and guilt and separation—all grave consequences. Paul writes that we are to "hate what is evil; cling to what is good" (Romans 12:9). As we take sin more seriously, we are far more apt to seek God's help to avoid its entrapment. An increasing aversion to sin accompanied by humble yieldedness to the Spirit magnifies the saving presence of Christ.

Perhaps we are slow to solemnly consider these issues because we are frightened of failure. If we indeed take God seriously and our increased efforts only bring repeated defeat, would we not be better off settling for mediocrity? Couldn't we just hold on to a few pleasurable sins and still serve God?

True, there is no condemnation for those in Christ and in this we rejoice. But God's great goodness and love should propel us to treat sin and his holiness seriously. He has given his all for us, shouldn't we in turn withhold nothing from him? Shouldn't we hate what he hates and love what he loves?

The good news is that God helps us to develop a distinct distaste for evil and a true thirst for holiness. "For the grace of God . . . teaches us to say 'No' to ungodliness and worldly passions, and to live self-controlled, upright and godly lives in this present age" (Titus 2:11–12). The sanctifying work of the Holy Spirit daily delivers us from the power of sin and fills us with power for holy living.

The God who calls us to holiness will make us holy.

———— • ————

I have so much to learn about your holiness, Lord. I tolerate certain sins in my life, and I ask you to help me see them as you do and by your grace help me to repent. I want to be serious about your work in my life because I want to see more of you. Examine my heart and lead me in your highway of holiness.

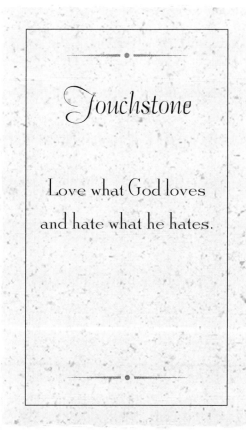

Touchstone

Love what God loves
and hate what he hates.

Each of us should please his neighbor for his good,
to build him up.

ROMANS 15:2

Your Serve

⸺⸺⸺ ❖ ⸺⸺⸺

There are episodes in our spiritual journey when we become spiritually stale. Our prayer life is flat. Our sense of God's presence is dulled. We have all been there and we all know how feeble our attempts to invigorate our spiritual heartbeat can be. We pray harder, we read the Scriptures longer, but to no avail.

May I suggest something quite practical that I have discovered: Find someone you can serve. There are, of course, many reasons why we occasionally find ourselves in a spiritual funk, but practicing a servant spirit can frequently be just the remedy we need.

C. S. Lewis wrote that "mankind is one vast need." We don't have to look far do we? There is an elderly neighbor who would love to have someone mow their grass or visit them. There are some kids at the local school who need a tutor. There are a few church members who can't afford minor car repairs.

Acts of pure service are wonderful ways to get our minds off of ourselves. The Scriptures exhort us to consider the interests of others above ourselves (Philippians 2:3) and serving those around us is an immensely practical means to fulfill this command. We are often so absorbed in our own problems, that the only way out is to concentrate on the needs of others. It is amazing how our perspective can change when we reach out and serve someone.

I think one reason is because we are never more like Christ than when we live with a servant's heart. Jesus, Lord of all, came to serve all. He "made himself nothing, taking the very nature of a servant" (Philippians 2:7). The more we serve in Christ's name, showing his love and compassion, the more Christlike we become. Serving others is always a matter of humbling ourselves, laying aside our rights. This process of humility is the primer for receiving fresh waves of grace. "God opposes the proud but gives grace to the humble" (James 4:6). And isn't grace—the incredible free flow of God's goodness and mercy—just what we often need to rejuvenate our spirits?

Think about this statement: We serve the Lord Jesus Christ by serving others. We encourage the fainthearted. We build up the weak. We take up the towel and demonstrate the love of Jesus Christ.

I think we enter the joy of our Master on earth by embarking on a lifestyle of spirit-led servanthood. Good deeds, empowered by the Holy Spirit, can resurrect our spiritual listlessness with might from heaven. Give it a try.

————— ◆ —————

I am often so encased in my own troubles, Lord, that I seldom think of the needs of others. Show me someone whom I can serve with your help that will bring them your joy and hope. I trust you will revive my spirit in the process and lead me into new praise and thanksgiving for your presence in me.

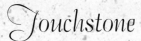

Touchstone

We are never more
Christlike than when we
serve others.

My Presence will go with you, and I will give you rest.

EXODUS 33:14

Don't Leave Home Without It

*D*espite their wanderings and spiritual vacillations in the wilderness, the Hebrews were continually cognizant of the presence of Jehovah God. By day, the Lord had manifested his presence by a cloud; at night, his presence was evidenced by fire. Every Israelite had visible proof that God was with them.

Following the debacle of their idolatry while Moses was receiving the Ten Commandments on the mountain, a crisis of epic proportions occurred. The people were punished for their grievous sin with loss of life, a severe plague, and the certainty of future judgment.

As harsh as these penalties were, the worst pronouncement came when the Lord spoke to Moses: "Go up to the land, flowing with milk and honey. But I will not go with you, because you are a stiff-necked people and I might destroy you on the way" (Exodus 33:3). Upon hearing the Lord's declaration to remove his presence, the people instantly went into mourning. Of all the possible consequences to their sin, the thought of living apart from God's presence was terrifying.

For Moses, the idea of leading several million bickering Hebrews without the comfort of Jehovah's presence was devastating. "If your Presence does not go with us, do not send us up from here" (Exodus 33:15). Moses knew the task would be impossible apart from God's constant presence.

Besides, Moses knew that it was the very tangible presence of Almighty God that differentiated the Hebrews from the pagan nations that stood in their way on their slow journey to Canaan. "How will anyone know that you are pleased with me and with your people unless you go with us? What else will distinguish me and your people from all the other people on the face of the earth?" (Exodus 33:16).

Today, the presence of the risen, ascended Christ in the life of the believer is the truth that sets us apart as his own. It is the presence of the Savior that gives us courage and faith to continue when the road is unsure and uncertain. It is the presence of the Lord that causes our hearts to swell with joy and peace in turbulent times.

We are sometimes apt to think that it is our talents or training that somehow differentiate us from the world. We might like to ascribe our successes to our knowledge of Scripture or certain disciplines. We must never make this kind of tactical mistake. It is the presence of the Holy Spirit that marks us as God's own and infuses us with the right stuff. Without his stamp of ownership and daily guidance, we all, like sheep, go astray.

The Shepherd and Guardian of our souls, Jesus Christ is the one who is with us forever. This is the good news of the gospel.

———— ❖ ————

Lord, keep me from dashing out and making my own plans without your guidance. I know that you are my ever-present God who is with me to teach me and guide in your ways. Your presence is my strength, joy, and comfort as I live and work.

Touchstone

God goes with us that
he might lead us into his
purposes.

About the Photographs

———————— ❦ ————————

Each photograph in this volume was captured on a five-week visit to New Zealand in the spring of 2002. This trip has proven to be one of the most exciting and rewarding of all my photographic journeys.

A Touch of His Freedom: Meditations on Freedom in Christ
Hardcover 0-310-54620-6

A Touch of His Goodness: Meditations on God's Abundant Goodness
Hardcover 0-310-21489-0

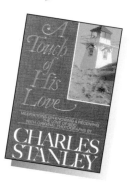

A Touch of His Love: Meditations on Knowing and Receiving the Love of God
Hardcover 0-310-54560-9

A Touch of His Joy: Meditations on God's Joy
Hardcover 0-310-21493-9

by Charles Stanley

A Touch of His Peace:
Meditations on Experiencing
the Peace of God
Hardcover 0-310-54550-1

A Touch of His Power:
Meditations on God's
Awesome Power
Hardcover 0-310-21492-0

A Touch of His Wisdom:
Meditations on the Book
of Proverbs
Hardcover 0-310-54540-4

ZONDERVAN™

GRAND RAPIDS, MICHIGAN 49530 USA

WWW.ZONDERVAN.COM

Pick up a copy at your favorite bookstore!

The Blessings of Brokenness
Why God Allows Us to Go Through Hard Times

Charles Stanley

Perhaps you've already experienced circumstances so shattering you may wonder today whether it's even possible to pick up the pieces. And maybe you can't. But God can—and the good news is, he wants to reassemble the shards of your life into a wholeness that only the broken can know.

Hardcover 0-310-20026-1
Audio Pages® Abridged Cassettes 0-310-20421-6

The Savior's Touch
Meditations with Original Photographs by

Charles Stanley

In this beautiful collection, pastor and best-selling author Charles Stanley illuminates eternal qualities of God's grace at work in our lives. *The Savior's Touch* combines four books by Dr. Stanley to present an anthology of insight into God's love, wisdom, peace, and freedom.

One hundred twenty-four probing, thoughtful devotions take us to the heart of Scripture for encouragement and direction on topics such as contentment, prayer, hostility, leadership, legalism, and other important and sometimes knotty issues that are part and parcel of Christian living. Through clear illustrations and pointed applications, Dr. Stanley guides us to the specific truths that lead to a richer life of faith.

Replete with the author's own striking photographs, *The Savior's Touch* is a treasury of life-transforming meditations by one whose camera artistry reflects his equally keen spiritual vision. This book will be a prized addition to the libraries of devotional readers and all who look to God's Word for answers to life's problems.

Hardcover 0-310-21037-2

Pick up a copy at your favorite bookstore!

ZONDERVAN™

GRAND RAPIDS, MICHIGAN 49530 USA

WWW.ZONDERVAN.COM